# *True Confessions*

Poems by
**Renee Norman**

For the Gee family,
one of my
favourite arts-
based family
friends

Renee

*inanna poetry & fiction series*

INANNA Publications and Education Inc.
Toronto, Canada

Inanna Publications and Education Inc.
212 Founders College, York University
4700 Keele Street
Toronto, Ontario M3J 1P3
Telephone: (416) 736-5356 Fax (416) 736-5765
Email: inanna@yorku.ca Web site: www.yorku.ca/inanna


Cover design by Val Fullard
Printed and bound in Canada


Library and Archives Canada Cataloguing in Publication

Norman, Renee, 1950-
True Confessions: poems / by Renee Norman.

(Inanna poetry and fiction series)
ISBN 0-9736709-2-4

I. Title. II. Series.

PS8627.077T78 2005    C811'.6  C2005-906643-1

# True Confessions

*For Sara, Rebecca, and Erin:*
*you are the sun, the stars, the universe of light*
*and for Don,*
*who stands with us in moonlight*
*and for my mother, Shirley Silver, who glows.*

# Contents

## I. This is How it Begins

## II. If I Call Myself

## III. When Geese Fly

## IV.  Giving Thanks

# I.  This Is How It Begins

# *Chop*

chop!
my mother dices zucchini
like a sushi chef
with a flourish
every piece small and tidy
uniform white nuggets
cut with green coats

migod, her shirt is on
inside out
she hasn't even noticed
the tag at the back
sticks out
its warning

duly alarmed
i watch her precise movements
as she sweeps vegetables into a bowl
is this how it begins?
and how do i handle this
without cutting into pride

without a word i turn my mother
who cries,
*what are you doing?*
i lift her shirt
off her shoulders
the way i undress my youngest child
when her head is stuck
my hands radiate
tenderness and humour

my mother laughs with me
at the adjustment made
exclaims:
*your damn aunt;*
*we went shopping,*
*she didn't say a word*

this is how it begins

# Calgary Storms

these summer visits home are
like waiting for the other shoe to drop
i am writing this on my old bed
in my old room
the furniture is now a table
stacked with coke bottles
an old bread basket
a broken flower arrangement

my mother shouts from the kitchen:
*come and get your daughter's dinner ready*
*i can't do everything*
she's mixing hot noodles at the stove
my daughter's seven
her dinner can wait for this poem

only a few weeks before i arrived
a black cloud opened up
shot hail the size of cannon balls
onto the streets
clogged the sewers

i will walk on new Berber rug
to help with dinner
flood rug we're calling it
i will swim upstairs  upstream
like a salmon
sensing my way

across the street
an old woman sits sideways in her car
feet out the open door she holds a hose
an arc of water sprays her lawn
it looks as if she is peeing from the car
like a man

the weather forecast calls for more rain
some hail
hot noodles
perhaps some new rugs
another shoe for sure

# I. *Photos at the Calgary Zoo*

I. Photos at the Calgary Zoo

such a feast for the eyes:

the male and female lions nap
in the grass
      large & sleek & powerful
a green tree snake wraps
itself around a branch
      leathery green knot
two bobcats follow one another
up & down a forest path
      like nervous parents who await a tardy child
      when one bobcat turns
      changes directions
      the other follows
      without ever looking
a gecko is stuck
upside down by its suction cups
on the side
of its glass container
      suspended in mid-air
the soft pink feathers of flamingoes
fan long thin legs
      poles so close together they merge
      one line of sight
a moose stands knee-deep
in muddy water
great antlers wide & heavy

II. Zoologics

the moose chews   sloshes   slobbers
        foliage caught between its silly-grin teeth
                        *at dinner a child gingerly*
                        *picks the chicken meat*
                        *off the bone*
                        *asks:  is this an animal*
                        *or a bird?*
                        *i avoid the answer*

powdered butterfly wings flutter
        slowly back & forth
a peacock lunges for his mark
        a crust of bread
his plumage shed
a long feather shaft drags
behind him
        a thin stick writing good-bye
        in the dust
one meerkat—alert
stands watch atop
the highest rock
        through the glass reflecting light

*a child finds a peacock feather*
*on the grass*
*& holds it to her cheek*
*she hears the flutter*
*of wings on nectar*
*the lion's roar*
*& touches the message*
*in the dust*

the male lion rises
rumbles a low-pitched roar
tosses his great red-gold-brown mane
at the fence

# Spotlight

too early
(for Jesus Christ Superstar at the Jubilee Auditorium)
I direct my husband
around the northwest of Calgary
trying to find my old childhood home
the big hill I remembered
driving up in the snow & ice
my mother's hands tense on the wheel
a silent signal of danger
Saint Andrew's church on the corner
across from prairie
my leg scratching brown weed & purple crocus
a gopher scurrying past
prickly tumbleweed toward
a slough where cows gathered to drink
the dirt road in front of our house
dries into a summer cake
pieces crack & lift up

past prairie on one side
& a hill of new houses on the other
I walked the lost Dutch boy home
his many relatives stared at me through the window
when I rang the bell again & again
didn't they know this was their child
I wondered
trying to explain to smiling bewildered foreign faces
when they finally opened the door

my husband drives & circles

the old neighbourhood divided
by a freeway
the prairie gone & Foothills Hospital
in its place

finally we find the block
my address still etched in my mind
1408-29 St. NW
chanted over & over like a skipping rhyme
in my head

it is no longer the same rhyme
confused
I look for the front window where I stood crying
when my mother left for work
the brick planter that held red geraniums in the summer
the driveway bordered by poppies & pansies
that cheered the Pontiac's ascent
the fenced back yard where I marvelled at cucumbers
which grew wild from seeds strewn by the garbage cans

1408 is not the same house anymore
& like the prairie has been rebuilt
a patch of my memories is overrun
with old weeds & dying gophers

suddenly I see the back lane
where I found those wild cucumbers
& the fence that let in small shafts of life
from the lane

## Dorian

if a face
records territory travelled
the lines spreading across the skin
like the tributaries that branched
from a deep river

why should i be shocked

i sat beside this old woman
did not know
the face
whose eyes had glinted once
as if she knew
all my secrets
could hold them in the irises
could shut them away behind the lens
with a smug smile

did not know a face is a map
that helps us find our way
read the routes we have taken

how could i forget
the images left
of where we have been
and who we are
fade
like a sepia photograph
over the years

my face a simulacrum
at home in the mirror
i look to see if i myself
had not turned
into an old ogre in the glass
some female Dorian Gray
comparing the graven image to the flesh

# Lunar Alignment

*for Rebecca*

under the orange glow
she explains to me
how the earth comes
between the sun and the harvest moon
how the moon slips
into earth's shadow
as i have slipped behind her
to view the eclipse from her eyes

she sounds like a Science textbook
i try to fix the facts
in my head as she pontificates
but the moon is mystery to me
an occasion for a poem
a reason to trek outside
with daughters
and stand in moonlight
my hands light upon her shoulders
our voices so clear in the night
a couple walking past
turn their heads and stare

you are the sun, the stars,
the universe of light
i am the harvest moon
absorbing whatever rises between us
as i stand in your dark night shadow
together we look for Saturn's rings
in a jewelled sky
i warm your back
this the most celestial motion of all

# Dog Day

*for Erin*

the dog lies in the same sunbeam
day after day
in this summer heat too
his curly black coat
blacker than hot tar

the clothes on the line
stiffen
creases glue sleeves together
tight
no air between the fabric
like summer tempers
fused

raspberries drop off the bushes
unpicked
hidden under weeds & brambles
scarlet spots that mark our languor

i empty torn knapsacks
& put away half-used scribblers
                broken crayons
                    wrinkled pictures

my youngest child dances with her paper body drawing
as if she knows
she is waltzing with a memory
*step*
she is dancing in the sunbeam
*step*
she is dancing in the space between the stiff sleeves
*step*
she is dancing all the fallen raspberries into wine
*step*
she is dancing so fast with paper shadows

# On the Horizon of Midnight

deep red camelias
stain the old tree outside my window
richly the splashes of color
relieve the never-ending grey
& full of green buds
the promise of more spring
long branches genuflect toward me,

dusk taking night
& pulling it over on incoming tide
the last break of light
between solid cloud
on the horizon of midnight

the blackening window reflects back
my chin double
someone becoming more invisible
dark through thick crisscrossed lines
of tiny leaf sprout
i watch the ocean suck up night

a faucet marking seconds
drips in a nearby sink
as if time can only be counted by water
the droplets siphoned from the ocean
rhythmical tap of tides

when full night descends
i wonder how i will ever get used to moving
in the world like a ghost
people no longer glancing my way
that mantle of invisibility
that descent of night

my daughters—red camelias
brush their hair like leaf manes
about their heads
the thick strands uncrossed
readying themselves for the parade
me behind them
fading into night

## On Vacation

*what do poets take*
*vacations from*
writes Robert Kroetsch
every piece of driftwood is a poem
every shell a lingering image
even with your eyes closed
words form tidepools
and barnacles on rocks
washed on waves of feeling

what do poets take
vacations from?
all the shores   caves   recesses   labyrinths
of the mind
collecting dross

## A Sting of Ocean

seagulls shriek like a mother scolding her children
the ocean accepts the color of a flawless sky
two sisters
a toddler on a homemade swing
flies across the briny smell of mussels, crab & sunfish
the tide a gluttony of liquid

i finger my swollen flesh where
the wasp has finally left its sting
for weeks the itch remains:
      venom, sand, words

## Spectrum

My words are colorless....What I can tell you, a
painter would show you.
I am only a poet, I am only a poor painter without
canvas without brush without palette.
      —Hélène Cixous in "The Last Painting"

can i write into color
the way the fading light shone on Golden Ears
casting snow covered peaks
into grey lined women wearing kerchiefs
or how the dirt dug up
for the new traffic light
froze into taupe hairbrush tufts
which needed washing

can i write into color
how the green rhododendron leaves
curled under
like they gave up
any hope of bloom or new life
and the way the moon
was surrounded
by a strange aura of yellow nightshine

can i write into color
the red ache i felt
as i walked up the hill
hearing the dogs howl out
messages to one another
and the blue sting on my cheek
as i turned it
from the recent coolness

can i write into color
the rust houses
rising up the distant landscape
a pattern of tiny monopoly board toys
placed near the sad tilt of evening sun
or my dark footsteps on the stone stairs
as I mounted them
to re-enter a world of white

## Repairing Damage

there are cracks in the foundation
of my parents' house
for years they've tolerated water
leaking in
during rainstorms barrels of water
pour in over the concrete patio
and steadily seep through the back door

the latest damage has been hard on my mother
she's tired of cleaning up spills
co-ordinating repairs
being at the mercy of the weather
it's made her irritable
quick to find fault in other structures

*don't play with the cupboard doors*
she tells my children
who should have known better
should have immediately hung the wet towels
after swimming
and the eldest should not be allowed
to wear lipstick the same color as mine
*i have to tell you* she says
in between clarifying what she meant
when she berated me
for allowing the youngest to phone an aunt
and leave a message
*she's 90 years old*
my mother reminds me
*she'll get confused*

*you're so jumpy* she comments
after the latest lecture
on not placing bottles in the bathroom garbage
the cause pinpointed for yet another
accumulation of water
only this time it turns out
the sink is leaking
the whole household
is letting my mother down

i tiptoe around her irascibility
she's 70
has problems with her eyes   ears
we all have to repeat what we say to her
*repeat what we say to her*
until i break
and fight back
fireweed erupting through the ruins
of a burnt forest
i defend the bottles
the towels
the phone message
the lipstick and
my lax parenting skills

a glacial silence descends
over all this disintegration
finally broken by the sound
of men in jeans with bare brown shoulders
drilling into the patio

and hauling pieces of old rock away
they're going to fill the cracks
recement the foundation

i marvel:
at the thickness of the jagged patio blocks
piled like small mountain ranges
which expose the black dirt underneath
stirred up by our footfalls
and hot summer prairie winds
at the way my mother makes my bed
one morning

## June Field Trip

my shoes sink
water from small sand holes
squirts up my leg
the ocean urinating upon intruders

children run between the tidepools
overturning shells and barnacle-encrusted rocks
in the hunt for sea life

a human fire hydrant
my hip hurts
i've had too much sun
i want to go home

the waves and the other mothers
come and go
come and go
*my mother died at 50*, one woman claims
her eyes like a lighthouse
upon her own daughter's wayward exploration
another takes snapshots:
brittany's boots overflowing with water
brittany finally daring to finger a live hermit crab
frantically i search my daughter's whereabouts
relieved when i spot her purple sunhat

she asks if it's all right to hold my hand
hers is sandy
she's tired too
we've both had enough of school mothers
photographs of children who disturb ecosystems
i receive her hand   sand and all
glad for the texture of granules

that slip through my fingers
abrade my skin
contrast to my thoughts:
deep June sadness
yet another ending

# For Sara at Twelve

you sat by me while i relaxed
in bathwater    no rubber ducks
launched around my thighs
no plastic ships
sailing through my legs
connected by your body
stretching into womanhood

12 years old today
you run your hands along the ceiling
leaving fingerprints    sticky with childhood
the length of mine
you chase the dog    for a hug
never quite catching
on to his game
but always second-guessing me
like a thermometer you rise and fall
your mercury held in my hands

you're not the mother
crabs your youngest sister
when you admonish her
the red lipstick i gave away
slashed across your lips
wax fire waiting to be heated by love

your face the one i know
from mirrors and pictures
the same knots tangle    your hair and mine
we both squint through
glasses spotted with breath

sometimes you *are* the mother
swirling as water
rubber ducks and ships
get suctioned into drains

# I.  *Mother's Madness*


I.  Mother's Madness

is this what you want them to remember?
the mud on the floor on the dress-up shoes
on the rug on the salamander on your face
the mother who rose up from the deep

the tension i'm sorry i'm sorry
a massive throbbing amoeba
crowding the room so viscous it spreads
like gel across the children
across the years i felt my own mother's anger
in the kitchen in the potatoes in the silence
i filled with worry about words unspoken

is this what you want them to remember?
stop running up and down the stairs
stop teasing your sister
stop bothering the dog
stop interrupting me when i'm working
stop stop stop
expecting me to be/hold
everything together in my hands
which are wringing words out of children
which are folding words into apologies
which are throwing words up into a barricade
STOP

is this what you want them to remember?

II. Out of the Fire and into the Frying Pan

for god's sake get a grip you
watched enough june cleaver brady bunch
        smile
        encourage
a salamander in time saves nine
good night sleep tight
don't let the children bite
to bed, to bed says mother head
after a while says it all
put on the ritz
put on the supper
there was an old mother who lived in a poem
1 potato 2 potato the 3rd potato looks like me
lullaby and good night

# True Confessions

what else is there to say about the ocean
mocha java
the teacher who used to climb a ladder
to an equipment loft at coffee breaks
and made love to the school secretary there
until the principal found them one day
shocking love all over the hula hoops

what else is there to say about blue sky
spaghetti sauce
the parents who knew their daughter
was making love with a boy in an upstairs room
when they brought home the groceries
it gave fresh meaning to the ripeness of grapefruits
and the softness of tomatoes

what else is there to say about geese floating in formation
souvlakia
the island wedding
everyone's pockets filled with pot-pourri
thrown after the ceremony
young lambs roasting on a spit
outside the lodge near the outhouse
nowhere to wash your hands
absolve yourself of the sins of the body
of the flesh
of the sacrifice to dinner

what else is there to say?
plenty
plenty

## II. If I Call Myself

# House of Mirrors

in a bedroom stands
a full-length mirror
it distorts the truth
somehow elongates your frame
like a fun house of mirrors
shows you slimmer
like toffee pulled thin

before the mirror
a 70 year old woman criticizes:
this is false

before the mirror
a new mother fingers
her slack emptied flesh

before the mirror
head turned as if on backwards
to glimpse the view from the rear
a schoolgirl asks:
do i look all right?

we are born in skins we don't choose
astonished when messages
are reversed in the glass
e z a g   s r e t t a m

when someone Jewish dies
the mourners cover all the mirrors
in the house
stark grief reflected back
in others' faces
you don't want to see your self
when the soul leaves a body

advice to schoolgirls:
cover the mirrors for a week
at least
mourn the body
in it
when it shatters

## On the Tongue

we are legion
        women
in middle age we sit
in the front rows of university classrooms
or performance halls
bury our faces in our hands
when Nicaraguan poet Daisy Zamora recites
a poem about her mother
when mature students read personal narratives aloud
—one mother's lost child is each particular sadness—

we are legion
        we women
listen to words we often do not voice aloud
so thick they are
on our tongues
pickled like cow parts
weighted down by our years

it's not that we want to keep silent
        women in middle age
no, the words always thunder in our ears
a waterfall rush that never seems to clear

it's just that
        when other women
recall our pain
we feel less alone
can really taste the salt in our tears
& lick our scars with their lightened tongues

## The Truth Is

*Truth is a woman*
Nietzsche wrote
and it wasn't a compliment either

Nietzsche must have dressed her
in chameleon
seductively because her siren eyes
signal immutable depths
Nietzsche must have drawn her
mother to fragments
daughter of deception
sister to suffering
singing a sharp lullaby
that pierces our neck cords

i think Truth is a man
and i'll paint him in the silver
swords and shields
that reflect off the frost
on the ground
the beams that scatter
at the rainbow's refracting

i'll name him
father to the zenith
son of the horizon
brother to brokenness
and it's no compliment either

# Samson and Delilah Revisited

Samson rides his bicycle
to work
long hair blowing up
around his bearded face
shaded by tree fans
swaying in silent adoration

Samson lifts weights
on weekends
cracks his knuckles
to adjust his long sturdy fingers
his arms make you forget
to breathe

Samson doesn't wear a helmet
washes his hair daily
can be seen
at coffee bars
and nowadays shuns meat

Samson grew his hair long
again
sleeps alone
but sometimes dreams of haircuts
doesn't miss Delilah

She collects wigs   hairpieces
sharpens knives and scissors
waits in courtroom hallways
dreams
in soft tendrils
loose curls
snip

## I Hear of Another Man Who Leaves His Wife and Children for a Younger Woman

Ah, Desire
      and who will tuck the children into bed
      their stories read
      their futures now uncertain

The sweet and flowery draping
round her dark voluptuous body
winds in and out of hallways
      and who will look at me with longing
      hips spread
      a lifetime colored on my lips
      of the hatred unleashed

Oh, olive skin
hair like a black thatched roof
eyes that sear the world
      and who turns each night in bed
      to stare at the books no longer there
      the glasses gone
      that familiar gesture
      of pushing back his hair
      alive in the room
      as if his shadow stood
      filled in by the children's scribbling
      over there
      pushing back that hair

Ah, Desire.
You are a maiden without remorse
love without the breakfast dishes
a fast ride into the uncharted
In 20 years will you be me?

## Dusting Off Willie Loman

dirt coats my fingertips
the telltale ink of my neglect
one cover folded back
the spine deformed
like an old woman
with a humpback

i dust off willie loman
elevate him to the ledge
beside hamlet   king lear
death binds them
aristophane's clouds and birds
hover nearby
a character in search of an author
i am no longer waiting for godot
or afraid of virginia woolf

but i wonder
as i neatly stack the plays
rows and rows of speeches and utterances
which i have
lived-recited-read-memorized-acted-analyzed-enjoyed
where were all the women playwrights?
how is it that only now
over 20 years later
i finally notice
all these fine and passionate words
were written by men

willie loman understands
the volume of the old woman
her back bent in shame

# Remember Lot's Wife

stitched in German on a section of quilt
purpleblue embroidery scripting a human bible
sewn with time and cotton wildflowers
> *flee Sodom and Gomorrah*
> *don't look back all the*
> *salt in the world isn't*
> *worth one last glance*

the quilt unfolds into threads of proverbs
Lot's wife beside submissiveness above godliness
diagonal to cleanliness
> *don't look back the future*
> *is in the salt shaker*

how many women's hearts
fingered the proverbial cross-stitch warning
sister of 8 sisters    mother of a daughter
remember your aunt?
Lot's wife?
the way you look over your shoulder
when someone calls your name?
> *lots of salt there*
> *in that pillar just*
> *run your embroidery hand over*
> *the column and taste*
> *her rebellion*

if threads could speak...
if salt were granules of women...
if Lot's wife at least got to have a name...
if a quilt kept one cold...
if a text is a palimpsest of lives peppered
with salty needle pricks.........................................

## This Is Dancing

when i was a young woman
i sat at tables waiting
(oh, please ask me to dance)
so grateful if any male
released me from dancing in my head

most nights
i went home restless
my feet folded under another table
i never really danced at all

these days
we women dance with women
blood in our veins
unleashed
take our places on the dance floor
with the rhythm
of cougars who have sprung
legs
too long on hold
we soar
pounce upon the world
over the music

## This Is Madness

delusional, they announced
(dinner table psychiatrists)
recounting the story
of how she obsessively mistook
a friendly chat at a game
for more
of how she needed to drive
30 miles all the way to town
to pick up her glasses
of how she couldn't be trusted
with the children

institutionalized, they announced
(dinner table newsmakers)
you have to watch
the quiet, deep ones

from my corner I listen

        watch
        remember the details
        quiet,
        deep,
        write the poem:
        delusional

# Six Secretaries in Search of a Poet

CAST:
choruses of women
chanting the mantra of men
between school board walls

SCENE:
they are seated behind typewriters
desks and phones
the Computer Age is not yet part of the drama
private lives are suspended
in the schedules of male superiors

THE PLAYWRIGHT:
a poet

ENTER:      the main characters

Cathy:(neat haircut  pleasant features
               *Redbook* magazine look)
At 5:30 this single mother runs into the arms of a four-year-old
on a sidewalk outside a daycare.

Joan:       (puffy cheeks  weight gain obvious)
On her day off this young wife travels to a clinic
for hormone treatments
designed to aid conception.

Alice &
Margaret:   (austere demeanours
               behind the blaze of glasses)
At last two women speak: "No gum-chewing please; no radios
playing; smoke in the lounge provided for that purpose."
Then silence.

Only the sound of personal mail
throats slit with a letter opener.
Comments follow on see-through blouses.
Droll references to all these contents
chew  play  and smoke
on stage.

Pauline &
Marie:          (foreign Parisian accents of
                modern language doyennes)
An admonition: "Don't eat all the chocolate"
sounds like music.

ENTER:      the other women (minor characters)

One is dying of cancer
but continues to type.

One always dances too long
with the men at parties
but knows audio-visual

One has abandoned her husband
and children
but plans professional development

The action takes place
on the stairs
in the elevators
behind makeshift dividers
through office doors

Clack of typewriter keys

ring of phones click of heels zip of purses
the chorus organizes
types reminds schedules corrects
flexes deflects

Playwright's notes:  this could be a paper operetta
sung to an orchestra of trivial tasks

without the cast
the sturdy halls crumble

sets should be constructed with more than the paint
of love-hope-pain-devastation
weighted by all the dreams that light
the buttons on their blouses
the zippers on their skirts

all the women
EXIT

## *Woman Flees*

we talk of Virginia Woolf
Kristevan intertextuality
how to find time
for baking cookies and
driving daughters

our e-mail messages
form proposals
papers  poetry

quick cups of coffee or tea
steam between meetings
where poems are traded for essays
in mutual review
where our revulsion for the letter grades
our children must endure in school
is mixed with 2% milk and
counter-hegemonic practice

all this activity
a proclivity towards the future
this yearning for learning

fleas in the fur of university departments
we burrow in
leave small red itchy impressions
that have the shape of disappearing tires
the smell of burned cookies

# M(other) of the Text

the blank page
no *tabula rasa* this
but white space
Monique Wittig's workshop
to play with text
sub/text inter/text
      words sounds images
      voices visions
in/scribed upon the blankness
even the silence
is a mirror
cr(eat)or of page
      entered c(entered) dec(entered)
a stage a re(e)al of film a canvas
(posit)ion of an in(strum)ent
collabor(ate)d in silence
trans(form)ed in text
b(ordered) by margins
no c(enter)
to the page
found wor(l)d
between the lines:
self
i/magined
for/gotten
re/membered
un/known
m(other) of the text
inter/dependent but separ(ate) too

I am a blank page
about to turn
to lift the page

# If I Call Myself

if I call myself a poet
will the words come
spilling upon that blank page
the blood of my memories

   if I call myself a revisionist
   will the changes come
   stories rewritten that mythologize
   a woman's experience

      if I call myself une féministe
      will my body come
      in an ecstasy of jouissance
      that celebrates my womanhood

         if I call myself a mother
         will my children come
         to remember back through me
         days we could have come together

            if I call myself a woman
            will I come to believe
            that I, too, live in a world
            that means to let me speak

if I call myself
will I come
screaming echoes of self
calling COME
            COME
               COME

## III. When Geese Fly

## The Queen of Between

deep in cyberspace
i tap out clever messages that
sizzle
my reluctance has given way to
full screen abandonment
i am naked but unseen
i am sultry in my
old jeans
i will say
anything be
anyone and
with a flick of
control x
i send waves of
emotion spiralling through
the net
entering  entering

internetting
i am the queen of
between
seduced by a computer
until the dog throws up
and cyberspace dissipates into
the rug cleaner
i rub circles with
my cloth wand
spreading oil on
water
coloring the
world with
foam
one reality

another
i am bent but willowy in
supplication
i will rub
anything be
anyone
i am the queen of
between
seduced by a rug cleaner
then the phone rings
and...

## No Smoking

his fingertips burnished
the orange-yellow of tobacco
he flips out yet another cigarette
the moment we leave the café
and pass the no smoking sign

he is philosophical he says
accepting the bad news he shares
with equanimity
apologetic he is taking so long
when i unconsciously finger my watch
aware of another imminent meeting

when we mapped out the last month of the course
we both remarked
*only days left, time goes so quickly*
such ruthlessness goes unnoticed

when we first met years ago
his eyes were the blue of icebergs
now turned gray
like his hair
like the rain-soaked day
like his news

he takes a long drag on a cigarette
whose smoke i follow until it disappears

# Cracked Pottery

all weekend i dropped objects:
my husband's $100 motorcycle helmet,
the lid to my mother-in-law's
Brown Betty teapot,
the word that ought to have followed a preposition

i was reaching:
for a boot which caused the helmet
to skid and land with a THUD,
for the lid which simply slipped
out of my hands,
for immortality in ink

i watched it all fly
in slow motion
knowing the ending before it hit
like watching a film fully foreshadowed

it's just a helmet
a lid
nouns
until the breakage
then objects animate with an afterlife
of wrath or grace
me scrabbling a weaponry of defence
my husband of course
temporarily unforgiving
a furious contrast to his mother's acceptance
that the lid was inexpensive
lasted longer
than ever she imagined it would

this morning the crows cawed
to one another from the housetops
they had been rummaging
through plastic garbage bags
picking turkey off the bones
sifting through scraps of cracked poetry
and dented debris
calling calling:
look past broken lids
which sometimes last longer
than ever we imagine they would

## *Never Eat Smarties Before Bedtime*

Zulu warrior with smarties in your eyes
you dance up and down the walls
blind with sweetness
clawing at the crusts of color
when at last you tear
the edible yellow button from one eye
a Hershey Cyclops
and stare at me in accusation
i cover my head
afraid i'll turn to sugar
Lot's wife in chocolate

## When Vacuums Fly

in 1961
Philip Jacobs rebuilt his mother's vacuum
so it flew
first prize at the Science Fair
also wrote morse code dashes in ink
all over the back of my favorite white dress
the designs of a genius
while i drew pimples
on a portrait of Mr. Ripkind
during our weekly half-hour of art
worried i'd have to ask him
for my first kotex
saw him half-smile when he passed by my desk
hurt outlined in his pock-marked face
a lesson in cruelty

and homely Joanie Dvorkin
came to me
declared she and Tommy were an item
i'd have to bow out
after years of our mothers crying: *machetunem*
whenever they met in shul
it would not be my first rejection

and Sarah Holtzman
wild Sarah Holtzman
whose mother spanked her with a wooden hanger
the wire ones had no substance
ran a black market pencil and eraser store
out of the teachers' stockroom at Hebrew School
played strip poker with her male cousins
made Dvorah who'd arrived from Israel
take off her top so we could see

her well-developed breasts
*you didn't have to do it*
i told Dvorah next day

as i wrote steamy entries
about red-haired Harry Holt
for five years in my five-year diary:
(today Harry squeezed me in a game of tag;
it felt good)

who knew then Becky would come
to my engagement party in leather pants
and a see-through blouse no bra
Sarah would leave her pearl ring
in an airport washroom
love a married man who left his wife
and three children then dumped her
Joanie's firstborn would be housed forever
in an institution
and i would have recurring dreams
about Jerry Goldfarb's house
where i'd never been
long after we went to prom
(i wore the same pink gown in every dream)
long after the year he died
(a brain tumor) while i was at university

36 years later in a school
Chris my student tells me
he likes to build and take things apart

Philip Jacobs rides again!

# Out of Web Site

i'm jumping the information highway
one web site after another
with a million other spiders
when i muse
how these webs
are nothing like the ones
we found in the forest
spider's lace, we named them
spun between so many leaves and trees
we lost count

on one a spider walked
the special tightrope of fine lines
laid down to allow it
entrance in and out of the maze
while others simply adorned the space
between the trees
waiting patiently
for something else to stick

from far away the webs on the ground
looked like fluff
blown from a flock of clothesdriers
only if we found the perfect angle
of light and shadow
on closer inspection
the intricate patterns revealed themselves

several webs hung askew
some lines adrift from interconnection
what mysterious web sights
these were

full of information only
fathomed by what was not

between 100 year old Douglas firs
long thin strobes of light flared
as if the sky held flashlights,
directed up and down,
on world wide webs
http
colon
slash slash
www
dot spider
dot com

# In the Bathroom Thou Shalt Eat Stones

*In the desert there is no sign that says, Thou shalt not
eat stones.*
                —Sufi proverb in *The Handmaid's Tale*
                by Margaret Atwood

in the bathroom at intermission
she fluffs her dyed blonde hair
she's gorgeous
i step aside
in the path between the stalls and sinks

the flower who primps with me at the mirror
a sleek willow dressed in black
who i don't yet know
is the same Nicaraguan poet
who once fled with her poems
in a backpack
exiles look different on PBS

we smile shyly
our eyes meet
in a Hallmark moment
this is the bathroom, after all
and a woman who has eloquently spoken
of how she continually
put her family at risk
by writing out
is free to check her appearance

*a woman once told me my poetry is too harsh*
she's telling the audience by the time I realize
i escaped from a crowded bathroom
with Daisy Zamora

*this poem is for that woman*
Daisy begins
ends:
*a woman who eats bonbons*
*while i eat stones*

O, Daisy
there is no sacred sweetness
in chocolates
for any woman
and stones like hairdyes
come in many shades and sizes

we all sound harsh in the mirror
have reflections weighted
with monumental poems

# New Westminster

I.  Between the Walls, Dead Mice

in a navy wool coat
she unlocks her first front door
from out of nowhere
the realtor appears
solicitous  apologetic
she longs to be alone
to take the first steps
without his sleazy regard
& only her unfriendliness
at last drives him away

the neighbour's son comes next
to offer help with boxes
she doesn't yet know
he will move away from his father's drinking
from his father's red-eyed watchfulness
with a shotgun
their bathroom window always open
too close to the back deck
she can hear this father cough
fart, pee, puke, aim
eventually she crosses all that out
with a lattice fence
the crisscrosses so close
not even light can pass through the tiny pinpoints
wood embroidery with a purpose

but that becomes the future past
this is the poem's present
when she does not realize
as she walks the echoing tiled hall

as she climbs the too-narrow stairs
to the attic rooms
childless
exactly who is empty
the self walking over red tiles
glued over self
grasping a shaky bannister
to find nails in between the grass
of the old shag rug
someone must have left them there
like leghold traps in the woods
when the vacuum floated over the shag
it would gulp one
seize up & die
the plug chewed away
by the venom of that careless leaving

whose stories gather like a hairball
in the corner of a broken tile?
bleed in the tip of a rusty nail?
linger in the smell of stale cigarette smoke
the yellow piss on blue rug
dead mice listen for them with skeletal ears
between the old walls
where termites slowly eat their way
into homelessness
while lovers lie on shag beds of nails
feel the cold metal nakedness
of empty rooms  empty hearts

she fills the living room with a bed
a fridge
the rug displays an orange juice stain

near the bedsheets
when florists peer into windows
see hardwood peeled back like orange skins
they assume no one lives there
as if only rooms of fine furniture & curtains
cribs
can breathe life into old houses
the gift enclosure card
sympathy for your loss
found wet by the curb
the only sign that someone sent cut flowers
to furnish all the emptiness

II.  Outside, Trees & Hedges

in the strawberry patch she pulls weeds
aborts bean plants
which would have produced a second crop
if she'd known they had more in them
could carry to a second term
if he hadn't shouted from the bathroom window
yes, pull them
it's a lot of work, isn't it?
and are you building that fence because of me?

around the Japanese plum tree
ants swarm
more ants than she has ever seen in one place
some trees in the neighbourhood have trunks
painted white
the ants avoid these
have gathered here for a conference
(did she build that fence because of us?)

the plums are delicious
she feeds her swelling belly with their red flesh
until she can't taste the embryo in pieces
until she can't hear the dotted lines of ants
or see him carrying empty bottles out of his house
returning with brown bags bulging

over the hedge which divides
another part of the yard
a small girl swings
feet in the air
her mother clanks around in the kitchen
directs the girl in for supper
with a spatula
can be heard screaming over an expensive ring
the girl lost
this ring is ruby with 2 small pearls
dropped in the grass somewhere
a bright strawberry waiting to be picked

beyond the hedge
a woman in a wheelchair
hangs wash on a low clothesline
2 dish towels  1 baby bib
& a pair of men's shorts
her husband an ex-priest
looks over the hedge daily
checks the spaces in the lattice fence
the meat on the BBQ
the garden
& her swelling belly
one day he chops down the thick hedge
in a massacre of leaves

it is an unholy act
when the baby is born
the ex-priest exclaims over her fine features
the man who carries bottles & shotguns
does not notice the squalls of a newborn
& the ring
a thoroughfare for the ants
remains lost
in the middle of the neighbourhood

# Fiftieth Anniversary Waltz

Grace and Jim have turned and turned
for 50 years dancing
  "through war"
the speeches avow
  "children, illness"
you could laugh or murmur
at all the right places
without even hearing the words
  "grandchildren"

Grace smiles
pirouettes under Jim's arm
Jim jokes
Grace wipes a tear away

in the kitchen Grace
fills tart shells with lemon sauce
one spills over and
she passes it to me
i love Grace's lemon tarts
the way she squirts out
a dollop of whipped cream on each tart
the tear she wiped away

# Lottery

year 5766 and the moon
blows in a new year
a time to think upon
all we've done/become
then God the scriptures say
decides the roster
for the coming year
atone and pray for forgiveness
it'll put you in the asset column

Yom Kippur
the Day of Atonement
a good myth
makes you try a little harder
pull up those socks or weeds
or skeletons
pray the deficit out of the ledger:
forgive me for the rituals
i abandoned long ago
the unwritten letters
don't cares
unkindnesses
too self-awares

God's nodding:   yeah, yeah
i know, i know
get to the adultery
abuse
assassination
all the good stuff
and that's just the a's

God's reading the local newspapers
feet up on an airtight reclining chair
calling: *Yitzchak, come and read this!*

or God, holding hands with the smallest angels
who teach the Holiest of Gamblers
the game of marbles
they explain to God
the exquisite pain of their passage
earth to fire
dust and ashes spraying
as one ruby agate hits another
sends it shooting through the universe

# Upon Learning of the Death...

you        electric
dressed as Mozart said
how ignorant they all are
sang
Yellow Submarine off-key
wrote
long nasty notes left in mailboxes

you        staking territory
stood alone
at the back of a school gym
yearly placed cut flowers
at the site where your daughter died
drunk
the scent of death
in your nostrils

you        a self-proclaimed world expert
on harmonies
rotted
from within while spring cancer grew
to a summer bloom

i        could feel
relieved or
nothing much at all
keep thinking
of the perspiration stain
at the back of your wool dress
your stomach
jutting out slightly in the front

### Earthquake at 9pm

seepeetza beats a drum
the story of owl
spreads its wings in the room
and the ghosts of the children lost
to this human-turned-animal
brush by the tiny hairs on my ear
and whisper a sad greeting

in the longhouse wolf and raven
stand on guard
while coyote's tricks amuse the child-ghosts
who have followed me here on my shoulders
like the feathers of wounded eagles
the children's laughter is stained red
and does not flutter

outside
the plates beneath the earth's surface
shift and groan
a wave of memory buckles the ground
gathers the child-ghosts
into the embrace of its curvature

owl hoots between the cracks of air
*hiss*
wolf howls in the fissures
an echo caught and carried further
together raven and eagle
fly the small ones
back to their mothers
yet the burden on my shoulders is heavy
the earthquake in my heart
only just beginning

## When Angels Follow

the presence of angels on your arms
reminds me to listen
to more than what is being said with words

written with the ink of nightshades
deep within our memories
banners bright with slogans unfold from wings
i read them as we speak

i must decipher sentences
confused by code
while you rest in the soft scent
of an unsung hymn

oh, how letters sometimes seem like irons
that brand my skin
with hot heaven

# In Benign Remembrance

the sun
a medallion of light
in a mohair fog
warm on your feeble knees
fuzzy with the memory
of that jacaranda tree
on African soil
the day your husband died
miles away
and you felt free
the touch of young girls' hands
upon your own
a father's newsprint stamped forever
in your brain
a mother's poetic legacy
written over with a woman's lot

i lived with you three days
until you died
swirled like the fog
among the chapters of your life
wondered:
how did Gina die?
and what about your son, Peter
daughter, Marcia
as you sat in that nursing home
a grey fog
on your knees
in search of a sun
a drop of benign remembrance

the newspaper eulogized
a matriarch of poetry
equal in scope and talent
to an earl
the mother of us all
you were not about to go forgotten

this fog
the sun
your poems mist
on my cheeks
where your words burn now

*Dorothy Livesay died December 29, 1996,*
*as I was reading her memoirs.*

## How the Dead

but that's how people die, he said
a military doctor
he knew death
had seen it countless times
now wrote it into story
the woman character who dies of cancer
gets a scant paragraph when she expires
and i complain
she dies with barely a word

that's not how people die

they die asking for fresh sheets on their beds
in diapers that need changing
with secrets thrush-heavy on their tongues

they die with diaries locked away in filing cabinets
the key between the pages
of *The History of the World*
dryers full of washed underwear
permanently stained
and half-eaten chocolate bars
tucked away in night table drawers

they die in front of parents
despite lovers
afraid to fall asleep and never wake
on the exhalation of a breath

they die in the middle of heat waves
snowstorms
during the hour we set the clock back every fall
when children cover themselves
with fallen leaves windswept into instants

# When Geese Fly


the 11 o'clock news:

in a campground
a young 11-year-old girl
was

when geese fly in v's
they are like punctuation marks
stop your gaze
in the text of blue sky
catch the eye
with the possibilities

my daughter read
that when geese fly in formation
they leave a space in the line
for the geese that died

in the fall
when the geese fly south
when the children return to school
i will look for
      the gaps       in
the        line

these gaps are like the words
i have crossed out of the lines
of this poem
xxxxxxxxxxxx
victims of my verbal gunshot
*wham!*
a word goes
a goose
a girl
all we hunters
making our marks
11-year-old commas
transform to periods
full stops

# IV. Giving Thanks

## After Reading Sharon Butala's *Perfection of the Morning*

no dream coyotes in my dreams, no
wonderful visions that i ponder
through the years just
long cloudy waits in grotesque hospitals
ghoulish interns who grab me and
oversize hypodermic needles stuck
in wool walls bent
unbearably

what possible direction to my life
could my bizarre  bleak
boring images hold instantly
forgettable my reveries arise
out of an immunized life
visits to schools and doctors
an occasional terrible nightmare
of lost children who reach
out of castles crying

the perfection in my morning contained
in suburban skies a pink tinge of snow
on mountains i see beyond
a landscape of chore

here the real coyote devours
pet cats  toy poodles
stalks the neighbourhood
like me
hungry
a stranger to dreams

# Kindling

red blue yellow tears
down the gilt-edged brass menorah
& a thread of snuffed smoke winds
wildly upward
the spirit grasping

through the eye of the flame
faces
dream of the future
candles
illuminate a past
2 triangles
that overlap the light

in the minor key
of a Hebrew blessing
corpses dance to bone
flesh
the clack of freedom sticking
to teeth
like overchewed gum
hands raised in madness greeting
hail  heil  hail

when the taste of oil
assaults the tongue
the redolent smell
a cloud of generations
hangs
holding dark moustaches
lost children
through the eye of the flame

# My Father's Shoes

no one could fill my father's shoes
thousands of pairs ordered & arranged
in rows for 48 years
his office always upstairs
at the top of buildings
once he walked through
a large piece of glass
he didn't notice it laid sideways
clear but treacherous
my father in a hurry
bounding up the stairs
he now climbs with a cane

no one could fill my father's shoes
the order forms
all in an accordion file folder
*how's business* i always ask
when i phone
a reflex question
from years of opening boxes like presents
to see the shoes within
read the fanciful names for styles
try on leather dresses for toes
transform feet to people with personalities

there are many ways
to walk through plate glass windows
we don't always see a warning reflection
at the top of the stairs
& even rows & rows of shoes
my father's shoes
won't keep broken glass from cutting

## The Long-Handled Fork

long strips of noodles dry
the dining room table a lattice
a screen door slams as we run in and out
my grandmother pokes a chicken
boiling in the soup pot
her long red-handled fork piercing its skin
small eggs harden in the broth
later my cousins and i will fight
over who get to eat those eggs
hard yellow balls dissolve in your mouth
in those days we never thought
about dead chicks or pregnant chickens

i sat at that long table set for Seder
*ma neeshtanah halaila hazeh mecoll halailot*
why is this night different from all other nights
  too shy to sing the four questions
   the year i was the youngest my face reddened
   all eyes on my indecision until my mother
   (impatient with my games)
  broke the hold with a slap
don't shirley, implored my grandmother
poking her red-handled fork
into more than chickens stewing

when i left home i took that fork
after my grandmother's heart had stopped
(always a complainer
no one listened to her complaint:
the ache in her chest)

at the airport the fork posed

a great security risk
the attendant tossed it
carelessly
into a box large enough for a table
as if he somehow knew
this was no mere fork
the box chock-full of ghostly noodles
   phantom yellow eggs
     fictive footsteps

i use that fork in my own kitchen
the red paint peeled off
the handle down to the plain grainy wood
as my children run in and out
the slam of a door
a skitter past long-handled forks
that pierce the skin of more than chickens
the ache in my chest

## Eagles Are Known for the Power of Flight and Vision

I.

she is drawing eagles in her sketch book
*(the present I like the best)*
occasionally she erases a wing
a beak  a talon
dissatisfied with a line or shading
as the eagles spread chimerical feathers
upon the page
a mother perched upon a branch
a smaller eagle flying back
the young returning to the nest
a reverse order of things

will she erase our last shouting match, too?
trace in the perspective of our hug
when finally, relieved
both of us retreated
aware that our intensity was overdrawn

II.

as she sketches to calm herself
before a pianoforte exam,
alighting beside her
another in a long lineage of performers
there to assist the perilous flight of talent
from the nest
i image a return

## A Fork, A Slap, A Poem

my grandmother's fork
poking about in a poem
my mother wants a copy
she remembers
only part of this story
the outrageous:
my trying to get through airport security
with a weapon from her kitchen
and the slap
she doesn't recall at all

i soften it by admitting
i deserved it
but this is written through holes
like a wood table
showing through a lace tablecloth
the wood makes its own pattern
which you see both separate from
& underneath the lace

one person stands in a pose
taking a picture·
behind her someone else
clicks the camera too
& behind the 2 of them
a 3rd lens records
the record of a record
a fork poem
stirs a poem about a poem

my mother muses
about how careful a mother should be
how slaps leave imprints on our children
*but you know that*
she reminds me
*you have your own*

my own
standing behind me with their cameras

# The Stability of Stairs

slowly up the stone stairs
i would help my *bubby*
my hand on her arm
my narrow T-straps
beside her ankles bulging
out of old lady shoes

up to my *zeda*
who was probably fixing a backed up sink
or feeding his chickens out back
maybe collecting rent from the DP's
exotic initials to me
who understood their meaning
in the strange food odours i breathed
thick in the air
in the Yiddish words i rolled on my tongue
a gibberish which tickled

i ran down linoleum halls
pockmarked from heels
hoping to catch a glimpse of the midget
at first my grandfather had just said:
*go away, little boy*

when i peered at the back porches
rising with clotheslines that waved
underwear flags of foreign soil
i knew other worlds existed
as surely as those
couched in my mother's warning:
*don't use too much toilet paper*
*or your zeda will get mad*

in the front room of my grandparents' apartment
the first suite by the entrance and the largest
a locked door led outside
but the stairs were missing
often i imagined myself opening that door
the white lace curtain gently parting
at my touch
pitching out into nothingness
my foot sinking down
                          down
desperately seeking the stability
of a stair
the way my grandparents and their tenants
must have reeled when they first arrived

how right it felt to steady my grandmother
if she swayed on the steps
i squeezed her arm
generations passing through my hold

## *Checking the Doors*

i open the car door and climb into the back seat
a cane lies across the floor
it hooks me in
my father has parked in the handicapped spot
a tag on the rearview mirror announces this new privilege

my mother looks over her shoulder as he drives
reads out road signs     gives warnings
  checks traffic flow
they banter back and forth
with the intimacy 47 years develops
my father snaps at my mother
when she makes one suggestion too many
and she grows cold and silent
the air crisp with belittlement
  and impatience
   change

my father makes his way to the front door
slowly with the cane
my mother and i carry in my suitcases
and he goes up to bed to rest
my mother solicitous about his pain
playing roles i am unaccustomed to viewing

my father forgets to lock the doors at night sometimes,
she tells me over tea
and it isn't so easy for her to leave anymore
he likes to complain to her, she adds
and gets tired now
a bowl of soup fills him

my father forgets to lock the doors at night,
my mother repeats to me
she has to check them herself
she listens for the one on the garage to close
when he's been out playing cards

who will check the doors when i get old,
my mother asks
clearing cups
hands marked with liver spots
the flesh on her upper arms
hangs loose like deflated water wings

i do not answer
i am struck dumb by doors flying open and banging shut
the echo of words i could not voice aloud
but wish i had:
      i will check them when you get old, mother
      i will check the doors

# My Father, Driving

I am sitting in the back seat
of the white Pontiac
on the way back from the hospital
(no children allowed)
but my father visited Uncle Mel
dying of cancer
and I only understand the sadness
in the car like an extra passenger:
we're giving a ride to Grief

I hear my father's words
*we hang onto life no matter what*
the way I am gripping
the upholstery of the front seat
in the days with no seatbelts
emotions flying all over the interior

it's pitch black
a Calgary morning in congested traffic
but at least the snow's abated
and the seatbelts are state of the art
my sister is driving my father to the hospital
there they insert a needle
through his shoulder to the tip of his liver
passing through a lung
I'm not in the car
not even in the city
and for weeks I have been talking to my father
through my mother
inserting care and concern in the phone lines
passing by the heart

when I finally speak to my father
I tell him I love him
pray for the best
listen to the dignity and courage
of words profound with 82 years of driving:
*what will be, will be*

someone comments:
*when you're that age every day is a gift*
I think the gift is a man in a white Pontiac
my father, driving
and I'm in the back seat again
holding on
holding on

## Giving Thanks

elated,
breathless,
on her weekly phone call
like a young girl
on her way to a first party
my mother sounds exactly like
she's having 10 guests
for Thanksgiving dinner
making lists so everything is perfect
on Saturday: make the stuffing
on Sunday: prepare the bird

the guest list includes:
a man who must breathe with oxygen at all times,
his lawyer son recently reinstated
after a suspension,
another man with Alzheimer's who may or may not
remember the turkey,
a widower who needs help making his bed,
without his son
(who was invited but forgot to decline
until my mother
irritated
doublechecked),
various wives with bad knees and caretaking skills
to their credit

i can taste my mother's mashed potatoes
know the menu will include her crisp coleslaw
the green and orange a match for the leaves
falling outside the dining room's bay window

i wonder which guest will request the wings
broken off the carcass,
which will love
my mother's grace and endurance,
who will give thanks
for that

# Acknowledgements

Some of these poems have appeared in their current or slightly altered form in the following periodicals and anthologies:

*Amethyst Review; Canadian Woman Studies/les cahiers de la femme; Canadian Writer's Journal; Child Anthology; CVII; Dandelion; Educational Insights; Freefall; Coastlines III Anthology; Green's Magazine; Inkshed; JET: Journal of Curriculum Theorizing; Journal of the Association for Research on Mothering; Kaleidoscope; lichen; Mentor's Canon Anthology; People's Poetry Letter; Potlatch Anthology; Prairie Fire; Prairie Journal; Room of One's Own; Roots Literary Magazine; Sandburg-Livesay Award Anthology; Saturday Review (Vancouver Sun); Teaching to Wonder: Responding to Poetry in the Classroom; Whetstone.*

•On page 30, Robert Kroetsch's words are from his book of poetry, *Seed Catalogue* (Winnipeg: Turnstone Press, 1986), pg. 35.
•On page 32, the quote by Hélène Cixous is from "The Last Painting" in *Coming to Writing and Other Essays*, Ed. Deborah Jenson, Trans. Sarah Cornell (Cambridge, MA: Harvard University Press, 1991), pgs. 104-106.
•On page 50, Nietzsche was cited by John D. Caputo in *Radical Hermeneutics: Repetition Deconstruction and the Hermeneutic Project* (Bloomington: Indiana University Press, 1987), pgs. 118-119.
•On page 77, the Sufi proverb quoted from Margaret Atwood's *The Handmaid's Tale* (Boston: Houghton Mifflin, 1986), appears in the preface.
•On page 99, Sharon Butala's *The Perfection of the Morning* was published in 1999 (Toronto: Harpercollins).

The photographs that appear on pages 11, 45, 65, 97 are from the poet's personal collection.

Renee Norman, Ph.D., is an award-winning poet, a writer, and a teacher. She completed her doctorate at the University of British Columbia in 1999. Her dissertation, *House of Mirrors: Performing Autobiograph(icall)y in Language/Education*, focuses on women's autobiographical writings, including her own, and on autobiography in language/literacy education, and was published as a book by Peter Lang Publishers, New York, in 2001. Renee's poetry, stories, and articles have been published widely in many literary and academic journals, such as *Canadian Woman Studies/les cahiers de la femme, Prairie Journal, Freefall*, and *English Quarterly*, as well as in anthologies and newspapers. She has received poetry and nonfiction prizes for her work. Renee is one of twelve Canadian woman poets whose poetry is featured in *The Missing Line*, published by Inanna Publications in 2004. Currently Renee teaches in a Fine Arts program in Vancouver School District. She lives in Coquitlam, BC, with her three daughters Sara, Rebecca, and Erin, and her husband Don.